Helen Orme is a successful author of fiction and non-fiction, particularly for reluctant and struggling readers. She has written over fifty books for Ransom Publishing.

Helen was a teacher for nearly thirty years. She worked as a Special Educational Needs Co-ordinator in a large comprehensive school, as an advisory teacher for IT and as teacher-in-charge for a pupil referral unit. These experiences have been invaluable in her writing.

# StreetWise

# Fixed It!

Helen Orme

Ransom

Street**Wise**

Fixed It!
by Helen Orme

Published by Ransom Publishing Ltd.
Radley House, 8 St. Cross Road, Winchester, Hampshire SO23 9HX, UK
www.ransom.co.uk

ISBN       978 184167 343 1
First published in 2014

# CONTENTS

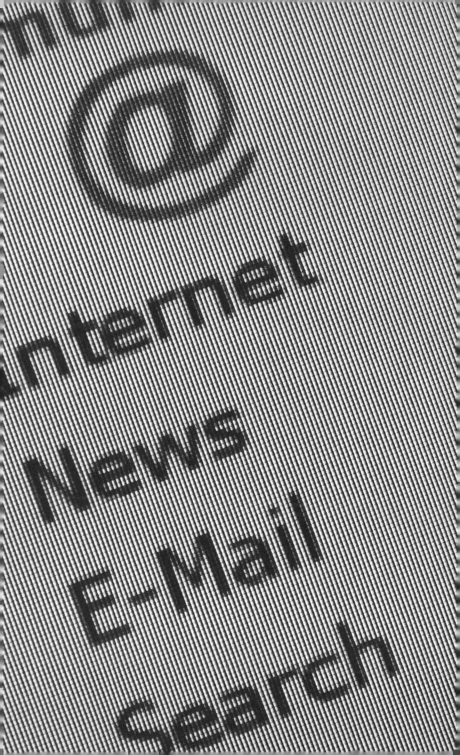

# ONE

## The Text

'Beep beep! Beep beep!'

Mrs Jepson was exasperated.

'How many times have I told you to

keep your mobiles switched off in lessons!

The head has warned you all. If it keeps

on happening, all phones will be banned

at school!'

Jasmine slipped her hand quickly into

her bag and switched the phone off. She'd

forgotten she had left it on. Somebody

must have sent her a text; she'd read it

later.

She got on with her work and tried to

look innocent, but that wasn't easy.

Lorna and Simon were grinning and

pointing at her, so that Mrs Jepson would know who it was.

She ignored them.

Between lessons, she switched on her phone and checked the message.

YOU ARE A STUCK-UP COW

She stood in the corridor, stunned. Who could have sent a nasty message like that?

'You all right, Jaz? Bad news?'

Tara had seen that she was upset. Tara was a good friend. They looked after each other.

But Jasmine couldn't bring herself to show Tara the message. She needed to wait until she had calmed down a bit.

'Tell you later.'

# TWO

## Ignore It

Jasmine showed Tara the message at lunch-time.

'Oh, Jaz, that's awful! Who sent it?'

'Don't know. The number's not in my address book.'

Tara checked her phone, but she couldn't find the number either.

'Ignore it, Jaz. Someone probably just put in the wrong number. It wasn't meant for you.'

Jasmine hadn't thought of that. Tara was probably right.

She felt relieved.

\*\*\*\*\*

Jasmine lived in a village out of town.

The school bus dropped her off at the end of her lane. It was a big, detached house with a large garden.

Jasmine knew she was lucky to live there.

When she got in, her dad was on the phone. She was really pleased to see him.

He spent a lot of time flying around the world and was often away. He hadn't been home for two weeks.

She rushed to give him a hug, but he held up his hand to stop her. An important call.

Jasmine was so pleased her dad was home, even though he spent the evening on the phone or doing paperwork.

She quite forgot about the nasty text. Until she got another one.

IM WATCHING U. JUST WAIT.

# THREE

## Someone's Trying to Get Me

It had arrived that evening, when

Jasmine was in her room.

She had just finished doing her

homework and was looking at posts on

the social networks she used.

Some of the people she was linked with were from school; then there were members of her family, and other people she didn't know.

She guessed that they must be friends of her friends. She was always careful with what she posted about herself – you could never be sure.

Tara was online, so Jasmine messaged

her straight away.

'Had another one. Someone's trying to get me. Any ideas?'

A minute later, Tara's reply arrived.

'Think I can guess. Bet it's Lorna. Talk tomorrow. T.'

Lorna! Of course! It was bound to be her!

She was always going on about Jasmine being posh. As if it was her fault

...riend

...peech: noun

...n: **confidant, companion**

...yms: acquaintance, ally, alter ego,

...iate, bosom buddy

...end

...rts of Speech: noun

...Definition: **benefactor**

...Synonyms: accomplice, adherent, advocate,

...ally, associate

**acquaintance**

Parts of Speech: noun

Definition: **a person known informally**

Synonyms: associate, association, colleague

that she lived in a big house!

But how could Jasmine prove it?

And what could she do to stop it?

# FOUR

## Fixed It?

The next day there weren't any texts, but then they started again.

Jasmine didn't want to turn her phone on any more. She thought about pretending she'd lost it and then getting her mum to buy her a new one with a different number.

Then on Friday afternoon she met up with Tara – who was looking pleased!

'Lorna left her mobile in the changing room. I handed it in to lost property – but I checked it out first. It's definitely her. She's got your number in there.'

'What am I going to do? If I report her for it, it'll only make it worse.'

'Jaz, I may have just fixed it. I removed your number from Lorna's phone and put another number from her address book with your name. She'll never notice the number's been switched. The next time she sends one of her messages, someone's going to be very surprised!'

'Tara, you're brilliant! Whose number was it?'

'Her mum's!'

# FIVE

## Not a Good Idea

Jasmine wanted Tara to come round to her place that evening. Tara had been a great friend and she wanted to make it up to her.

'Sorry, Jaz, can't tonight. I've got a date!'

'Fantastic! Someone I know?'

'Don't think so. One of the boys on that Internet site. Been on it for ages, so must be a friend of someone. Says he lives near. Exciting, eh?'

Jasmine felt a strange feeling inside. That couldn't be a good idea. Tara had helped her. Now she wanted to help Tara.

But how?

# Questions on the Story

◆ Why did Tara think Lorna was sending the texts?

◆ Why was Lorna picking on Jasmine?

◆ What idea did Jasmine have to stop the messages?

# Discussion
# Points

◆ Was Tara right to do what she did with Lorna 's phone?

What else could she have done?

◆ Why was Jasmine worried at the end of the story?

◆ You have a friend who has arranged to meet someone she or he met on the Internet.

What should you do?

# Activities

◆ Draw up a school rule for mobile phones in school.

◆ Lorna sends a rude message – to her mum!

Write an account of what happens when she gets home.

◆ 'People don't like being told what to do! They need to decide on their own rules for using social networking sites.'

What are *your* rules?